The Chronnoisseur

Edible/Topical Journal

www.lulu.com

Cover Design: Todd M. Schilling Design
Interior Design: Todd M. Schilling Design
Editor: Justin Klein
ISBN: 978-1-329-99723-3

The purpose of this journal is to chronicle the consumption of cannabis for individuals who like to enjoy the different flavors, aromas, and methods of consumption available. I hope this book will encourage people to savor the variation between different strains as well as the variations between the same strains from different growers and regions. This journal will be a means for you to note the flavors, appearance, method of consumption, as well as the overall experience you like the best and least. Utilize this as a quick reference guide to determine whether you would like a future choice in product, and whether that product has unbeknownst to you already been consumed by you in the method of which you are currently about to try again; because, let's be honest, sometimes we forget.

Enjoy Responsibly!

How to Fill Out

In the dispensary section list the name and/or location from which you purchased your cannabis. This will allow you to differentiate between strains in different regions and from dispensary/growers in the same region. The date section can be used as a reference to see whether the characteristics of your edibles/topicals, or even your palate, have changed over time.

Next it is important to list the strain name of the edible/topical you are tasting. Check whether the strain is an indica, sativa, or both for hybrid. The $/g section is meant for you to note the difference in prices between regions, dispensaries, and strains.

The next few sections are meant to help in describing the edible/topical prior to consumption. Utilize the blank bars under each heading to shade in the level of each descriptor written. The blank description area of this section should be used to elaborate on everything that the shading can not fully express.

These next sections will be used to describe the consumption of the edibles/topicals. Under the method section, circle whether you consumed the edibles/topicals through a baked good, topical, candy or tincture. Fill out the taste and flavor sections in the same manner as you did with the shading above. The blank description under this section should be utilized to elaborate on the type of method of consumption, as well as the characteristics of the taste and flavor.

The final section is to capture your overall impression of the edible/topical. Rate your overall experience on a scale of 1 through 10 and circle yes or no depending on whether you would recommend this to a peer.

Under experience you can describe what type of affect the edible/topical had on you and a story of something that may have occurred while under the influence of that particular strain, using that particular method.

The following page is an example of how to complete the pages of your journal.

		Date	7/15

Dispensary (name/location)   ABC Alt. Medicine - WA

Strain   75mg Raspberry Crumble   indica ✓ sativa ✓   Price   10 $~~6~~

Color
- Dark
- Light

Clarity
- Opaque
- Clear

Cannabis Scent
- Heavy
- Light

Pine/Earthy   Citrus   Skunk/Cheese   Floral

Description   Graham cracker crust with raspberry jelly topped with crumbles - no noticeable cannabis smell. Made with shatter.

Taste

Floral   Citrus   Cheese   Nutty   Earthy   Spicy   Peppery   Fruity

Cannabis Flavor
- Heavy
- Light

Description   Delicious! Made with real raspberries, slight cannabis aftertaste.

Overall   7 /10   Recommend   Yes No

Experience   Mellow, enjoyable high. Body high really kicked in after smoking.

Date _____

Dispensary (name/location) _____

Strain _____

indica ☐
sativa ☐

Price _____ $/g

Color
☐ Dark
☐ Light

Clarity
☐ Opaque
☐ Clear

Cannabis Scent
Heavy ☐ ☐ ☐ ☐
Light

Pine/Earthy | Citrus | Skunk/Cheese | Floral

Description _____
_____

Taste

Floral — Citrus
Fruity — Cheese
Peppery — Nutty
Spicy — Earthy

Cannabis Flavor
☐ Heavy
Light

Description _____
_____

Overall _____ /10

Recommend Yes / No

Experience _____
_____
_____

Date _____

Dispensary (name/location) _____

Strain _____ indica ☐ Price _____ $/g
                         sativa ☐

Color
☐ Dark
☐ Light

Clarity
☐ Opaque
☐ Clear

Cannabis Scent
Heavy ☐ ☐ ☐ ☐
Light
Pine/Earthy Citrus Skunk/Cheese Floral

Description _____
_____

Taste

Floral Citrus
Fruity   Cheese
Peppery   Nutty
  Spicy Earthy

Cannabis Flavor
☐ Heavy
  Light

Description _____
_____

Overall _____ /10 _____

Recommend Yes / No

Experience _____
_____
_____

Date _____

Dispensary (name/location) _____

Strain _____   indica ☐   Price _____ $/g
                                          sativa ☐

Color
☐ Dark

☐ Light

Clarity
☐ Opaque

☐ Clear

Cannabis Scent
Heavy ☐ ☐ ☐ ☐

Light

Pine/Earthy Citrus Skunk/Cheese Floral

Description _____
_____

Taste

Floral Citrus
Fruity   Cheese
Peppery   Nutty
  Spicy Earthy

Cannabis Flavor
☐ Heavy

Light

Description _____
_____

Overall _____ /10 _____   Recommend   Yes / No

Experience _____
_____
_____

Date _____

Dispensary (name/location) _____

Strain _____   indica ☐   Price _____ $/g
                                   sativa ☐

Color
☐ Dark

☐ Light

Clarity
☐ Opaque

☐ Clear

Cannabis Scent
Heavy ☐ ☐ ☐ ☐

Light

Pine/Earthy   Citrus   Skunk/Cheese   Floral

Description _____

_____

Taste

Floral   Citrus
Fruity   Cheese
Peppery   Nutty
   Spicy   Earthy

Cannabis Flavor
☐ Heavy

  Light

Description _____

_____

Overall _____ /10 _____   Recommend   Yes / No

Experience _____

_____

_____

Date _____

Dispensary (name/location) _____

Strain _____   indica ☐   Price _____ $/g
                      sativa ☐

Color   **Clarity**   **Cannabis Scent**

☐ Dark   ☐ Opaque   Heavy ☐ ☐ ☐ ☐

☐ Light   ☐ Clear   Light

Pine/Earthy | Citrus | Skunk/Cheese | Floral

Description _____
_____

Taste   **Cannabis Flavor**

Floral Citrus   Heavy ☐
Fruity   Cheese
Peppery   Nutty   Light
Spicy Earthy

Description _____
_____

Overall _____ /10 _____   Recommend   Yes / No

Experience _____
_____
_____

Date _____

Dispensary (name/location) _____

Strain _____ indica ☐ Price _____ $/g
                         sativa ☐

Color
☐ Dark
☐ Light

Clarity
☐ Opaque
☐ Clear

Cannabis Scent
Heavy ☐ ☐ ☐ ☐
Light
  Pine/Earthy Citrus Skunk/Cheese Floral

Description _____
_____

Taste

Floral Citrus Cheese Nutty Earthy Spicy Peppery Fruity

Cannabis Flavor
☐ Heavy
  Light

Description _____
_____

Overall _____ /10 _____   Recommend   Yes / No

Experience _____
_____
_____

Date _____

Dispensary (name/location) _____

Strain _____   indica ☐   Price _____ $/g
                                    sativa ☐

Color   **Clarity**   **Cannabis Scent**
☐ Dark   ☐ Opaque   Heavy ☐ ☐ ☐ ☐
☐ Light   ☐ Clear   Light
                                              Pine/Earthy Citrus Skunk/Cheese Floral

Description _____
_____

Taste   **Cannabis Flavor**
Floral Citrus   Heavy ☐
Fruity   Cheese
Peppery   Nutty   Light
Spicy Earthy

Description _____
_____

Overall _____ /10 _____   Recommend   Yes / No

Experience _____
_____
_____

Dispensary (name/location) _____

Strain _____

indica ☐
sativa ☐

Price _____ $/g

Color

☐ Dark

☐ Light

Clarity

☐ Opaque

☐ Clear

Cannabis Scent

Heavy ☐ ☐ ☐ ☐

Light

Pine/Earthy *Citrus* *Skunk/Cheese* *Floral*

Description _____

_____

Taste

Floral Citrus

Fruity Cheese

Peppery Nutty

Spicy Earthy

Cannabis Flavor

☐ Heavy

Light

Description _____

_____

Overall _____ /10 _____

Recommend Yes / No

Experience _____

_____

_____

Date _____

Dispensary (name/location) _____

Strain _____ indica ☐   Price _____ $/g
                                   sativa ☐

Color
☐ Dark

☐ Light

Clarity
☐ Opaque

☐ Clear

Cannabis Scent
Heavy ☐ ☐ ☐ ☐

Light

Pine/Earthy Citrus Skunk/Cheese Floral

Description _____

_____

Taste

Floral Citrus
Fruity   Cheese
Peppery   Nutty
  Spicy Earthy

Cannabis Flavor
☐ Heavy

Light

Description _____

Overall _____ /10 _____   Recommend   Yes / No

Experience _____

_____

_____

Date _____

Dispensary (name/location) _____

Strain _____ indica ☐ Price _____ $/g
                                  sativa ☐

Color   **Clarity**   **Cannabis Scent**

☐ Dark   ☐ Opaque   Heavy ☐ ☐ ☐ ☐

☐ Light   ☐ Clear   Light ☐ ☐ ☐ ☐

                                         Pine/Earthy Citrus Skunk/Cheese Floral

Description _____

_____

                                    Taste   **Cannabis Flavor**

                              Floral   Citrus   ☐ Heavy
                          Fruity   Cheese
                                                           ☐ Light
                        Peppery   Nutty

                          Spicy   Earthy

Description _____

_____

Overall _____ /10 _____   Recommend   Yes / No

Experience _____

_____

_____

Date _____

Dispensary (name/location) _____

Strain _____ indica ☐ Price _____ $/g
                     sativa ☐

Color   **Clarity**   **Cannabis Scent**

☐ Dark   ☐ Opaque   Heavy ☐ ☐ ☐ ☐

☐ Light   ☐ Clear   Light

                                            Pine/Earthy Citrus Skunk/Cheese Floral

Description _____
_____

Taste   **Cannabis Flavor**

Floral Citrus   ☐ Heavy
Fruity   Cheese
Peppery   Nutty   ☐ Light
Spicy Earthy

Description _____
_____

Overall _____ /10 _____   Recommend _____ Yes / No

Experience _____
_____
_____

Date _____

Dispensary (name/location) _____

Strain _____   indica ☐   Price _____ $/g
                           sativa ☐

Color
☐ Dark
☐ Light

Clarity
☐ Opaque
☐ Clear

Cannabis Scent
Heavy ☐ ☐ ☐ ☐
Light
Pine/Earthy Citrus Skunk/Cheese Floral

Description _____

_____

Taste
Floral Citrus
Fruity   Cheese
Peppery   Nutty
Spicy Earthy

Cannabis Flavor
☐ Heavy
  Light

Description _____

_____

Overall _____ /10 _____   Recommend   Yes / No

Experience _____

_____

_____

Date _____

Dispensary (name/location) _____

Strain _____ indica ☐   Price _____ $/g
                                         sativa ☐

Color	Clarity	Cannabis Scent

Color
☐ Dark
☐ Light

Clarity
☐ Opaque
☐ Clear

Cannabis Scent
Heavy ☐ ☐ ☐ ☐
Light
Pine/Earthy   Citrus   Skunk/Cheese   Floral

Description _____
_____

Taste

Floral Citrus
Fruity   Cheese
Peppery   Nutty
   Spicy   Earthy

Cannabis Flavor
☐ Heavy
☐ Light

Description _____
_____

Overall _____ /10 _____   Recommend   Yes / No

Experience _____
_____
_____

Date _____

Dispensary (name/location) _____

Strain _____   indica ☐   Price _____ $/g
                                 sativa ☐

Color
☐ Dark

☐ Light

Clarity
☐ Opaque

☐ Clear

Cannabis Scent
Heavy ☐ ☐ ☐ ☐

Light

Pine/Earthy   Citrus   Skunk/Cheese   Floral

Description _____

_____

Taste

Floral   Citrus
Fruity   Cheese
Peppery   Nutty
   Spicy   Earthy

Cannabis Flavor
☐ Heavy

Light

Description _____

_____

Overall _____ /10 _____   Recommend   Yes / No

Experience _____

_____

_____

Date _____

Dispensary (name/location) _____

Strain _____

indica ☐
sativa ☐

Price _____ $/g

Color
☐ Dark
☐ Light

Clarity
☐ Opaque
☐ Clear

Cannabis Scent
Heavy ☐ ☐ ☐ ☐
Light

Pine/Earthy Citrus Skunk/Cheese Floral

Description _____

_____

Taste

Floral Citrus
Fruity   Cheese
Peppery   Nutty
Spicy Earthy

Cannabis Flavor
☐ Heavy
Light

Description _____

_____

Overall _____ /10 _____

Recommend   Yes / No

Experience _____

_____

_____

Date _____

Dispensary (name/location) _____

Strain _____ indica ☐ Price _____ $/g
                                      sativa ☐

Color
☐ Dark

☐ Light

Clarity
☐ Opaque

☐ Clear

Cannabis Scent
Heavy ☐ ☐ ☐ ☐

Light

Pine/Earthy Citrus Skunk/Cheese Floral

Description _____

_____

Taste

Floral Citrus
Fruity   Cheese
Peppery   Nutty
  Spicy Earthy

Cannabis Flavor
☐ Heavy

Light

Description _____

_____

Overall _____ /10 _____   Recommend   Yes / No

Experience _____

_____

_____

Dispensary (name/location)

Strain

indica ☐
sativa ☐

Price _____ $/g

Color
☐ Dark

☐ Light

Clarity
☐ Opaque

☐ Clear

Cannabis Scent
Heavy ☐ ☐ ☐ ☐
Light

Pine/Earthy | Citrus | Skunk/Cheese | Floral

Description

_____

Taste
Floral / Citrus
Fruity / Cheese
Peppery / Nutty
Spicy / Earthy

Cannabis Flavor
☐ Heavy

☐ Light

Description

_____

Overall _____ /10

Recommend   Yes / No

Experience

_____

_____

Date _____

Dispensary (name/location) _____

Strain _____ indica ☐ Price _____ $/g
                                           sativa ☐

Color
☐ Dark
☐ Light

Clarity
☐ Opaque
☐ Clear

Cannabis Scent
Heavy ☐ ☐ ☐ ☐
Light

Pine/Earthy | Citrus | Skunk/Cheese | Floral

Description _____
_____

Taste

Floral | Citrus
Fruity | Cheese
Peppery | Nutty
Spicy | Earthy

Cannabis Flavor
☐ Heavy
   Light

Description _____
_____

Overall _____ /10 _____   Recommend   Yes / No

Experience _____
_____
_____

Date _____

Dispensary (name/location) _____

Strain _____   indica ☐   Price _____ $/g
                           sativa ☐

Color

☐ Dark

☐ Light

Clarity

☐ Opaque

☐ Clear

Cannabis Scent

Heavy ☐ ☐ ☐ ☐ Light

Pine/Earthy   Citrus   Skunk/Cheese   Floral

Description

_____

_____

Taste

Floral   Citrus
Fruity   Cheese
Peppery   Nutty
    Spicy   Earthy

Cannabis Flavor

☐ Heavy

☐ Light

Description

_____

_____

Overall _____/10_____   Recommend   Yes / No

Experience

_____

_____

_____

Dispensary (name/location) _____

Strain _____ indica ☐ Price _____ $/g
                                          sativa ☐

Color   ### Clarity   ### Cannabis Scent

☐ Dark   ☐ Opaque   Heavy ☐ ☐ ☐ ☐
                                  Light
☐ Light   ☐ Clear

Pine/Earthy *Citrus* *Skunk/Cheese* *Floral*

Description _____

_____

Taste   ### Cannabis Flavor

Floral Citrus
Fruity   Cheese
Peppery   Nutty
   Spicy Earthy

☐ Heavy

☐ Light

Description _____

_____

Overall _____ /10 _____   Recommend   Yes / No

Experience _____

_____

_____

Date _____

Dispensary (name/location) _____

Strain _____   indica ☐   Price _____ $/g
                            sativa ☐

Color	Clarity	Cannabis Scent

Color
☐ Dark
☐ Light

Clarity
☐ Opaque
☐ Clear

Cannabis Scent
Heavy ☐ ☐ ☐ ☐
Light
Pine/Earthy Citrus Skunk/Cheese Floral

Description _____
_____

Taste
Floral Citrus
Fruity   Cheese
Peppery   Nutty
Spicy   Earthy

Cannabis Flavor
☐ Heavy
  Light

Description _____
_____

Overall _____ /10 _____   Recommend   Yes / No

Experience _____
_____
_____

Date _____

Dispensary (name/location) _____

Strain _____ indica ☐ Price _____ $/g
                                   sativa ☐

Color   ### Clarity   ### Cannabis Scent

☐ Dark   ☐ Opaque   Heavy ☐ ☐ ☐ ☐

☐ Light   ☐ Clear   Light

                                         Pine/Earthy Citrus Skunk/Cheese Floral

Description _____

_____

                                    Taste   Cannabis Flavor

                           Floral Citrus   ☐ Heavy
                        Fruity   Cheese
                                                    ☐ Light
                        Peppery   Nutty

                           Spicy Earthy

Description _____

_____

Overall _____ /10 _____   Recommend   Yes / No

Experience _____

_____

_____

Date _____

Dispensary (name/location) _____

Strain _____   indica ☐   Price _____ $/g
                                     sativa ☐

Color
☐ Dark

☐ Light

Clarity
☐ Opaque

☐ Clear

Cannabis Scent
Heavy ☐ ☐ ☐ ☐
Light
Pine/Earthy Citrus Skunk/Cheese Floral

Description _____

_____

Taste
Floral Citrus
Fruity   Cheese
Peppery   Nutty
Spicy Earthy

Cannabis Flavor
☐ Heavy

☐ Light

Description _____

_____

Overall _____ /10 _____   Recommend   Yes / No

Experience _____

_____

_____

Dispensary (name/location) _____

Strain _____ indica ☐ sativa ☐ Price _____ $/g

Color
☐ Dark

☐ Light

Clarity
☐ Opaque

☐ Clear

Cannabis Scent
Heavy ☐ ☐ ☐ ☐

Light

Pine/Earthy Citrus Skunk/Cheese Floral

Description _____

_____

Taste

Floral Citrus
Fruity   Cheese
Peppery   Nutty
Spicy Earthy

Cannabis Flavor
☐ Heavy

Light

Description _____

_____

Overall _____ /10   Recommend   Yes / No

Experience _____

_____

_____

Date _____

Dispensary (name/location) _____

Strain _____ indica ☐ sativa ☐ Price _____ $/g

Color
☐ Dark
☐ Light

Clarity
☐ Opaque
☐ Clear

Cannabis Scent
Heavy ☐ ☐ ☐ ☐
Light

Pine/Earthy Citrus Skunk/Cheese Floral

Description _____
_____

Taste

Floral · Citrus · Cheese · Nutty · Earthy · Spicy · Peppery · Fruity

Cannabis Flavor
Heavy ☐
Light

Description _____
_____

Overall _____ /10 _____

Recommend   Yes / No

Experience _____
_____
_____

Date _____

Dispensary (name/location) _____

Strain _____   indica ☐   Price _____ $/g
                          sativa ☐

Color	Clarity	Cannabis Scent

Color
☐ Dark
☐ Light

Clarity
☐ Opaque
☐ Clear

Cannabis Scent
Heavy ☐ ☐ ☐ ☐
Light

Pine/Earthy *Citrus* *Skunk/Cheese* *Floral*

Description _____

_____

Taste   Cannabis Flavor
                ☐ Heavy
                   Light

Taste wheel: Floral, Citrus, Cheese, Nutty, Earthy, Spicy, Peppery, Fruity

Description _____

_____

Overall _____ /10 _____   Recommend   Yes / No

Experience _____

_____

_____

Date _____

Strain _____ indica ☐   Price _____ $/g
                             sativa ☐

Color
☐ Dark

☐ Light

Clarity
☐ Opaque

☐ Clear

Cannabis Scent
Heavy ☐ ☐ ☐ ☐

Light

Pine/Earthy   Citrus   Skunk/Cheese   Floral

Description _____

_____

Taste
Floral   Citrus

Fruity   Cheese

Peppery   Nutty

Spicy   Earthy

Cannabis Flavor
☐ Heavy

Light

Description _____

_____

Overall _____ /10 _____   Recommend   Yes / No

Experience _____

_____

_____

Date _____

Dispensary (name/location) _____

Strain _____ indica ☐ Price _____ $/g
                                 sativa ☐

Color   ### Clarity   ### Cannabis Scent

☐ Dark   ☐ Opaque   Heavy ☐ ☐ ☐ ☐
☐ Light   ☐ Clear   Light

                                  Pine/Earthy Citrus Skunk/Cheese Floral

Description _____

_____

                          ### Taste   ### Cannabis Flavor

                          Floral Citrus   ☐ Heavy
                       Fruity   Cheese
                                              ☐ Light
                      Peppery   Nutty

                         Spicy Earthy

Description _____

_____

Overall _____ /10 _____   Recommend   Yes / No

Experience _____

_____

_____

Date _____

Dispensary (name/location) _____

Strain _____   indica ☐   Price _____ $/g
                                 sativa ☐

Color   **Clarity**   **Cannabis Scent**

☐ Dark   ☐ Opaque   Heavy ☐ ☐ ☐ ☐

☐ Light   ☐ Clear   Light

                                                Pine/Earthy Citrus Skunk/Cheese Floral

Description _____
_____

Taste   **Cannabis Flavor**

Floral Citrus   ☐ Heavy
Fruity   Cheese
Peppery   Nutty   ☐ Light
  Spicy Earthy

Description _____
_____

Overall _____ /10 _____   Recommend   Yes / No

Experience _____
_____
_____

Dispensary (name/location) _____

Strain _____ indica ☐ Price _____ $/g
                                           sativa ☐

Color
☐ Dark

☐ Light

Clarity
☐ Opaque

☐ Clear

Cannabis Scent
Heavy ☐ ☐ ☐ ☐

Light

Pine/Earthy Citrus Skunk/Cheese Floral

Description _____

_____

Taste

Floral Citrus
Fruity   Cheese
Peppery   Nutty
Spicy Earthy

Cannabis Flavor
☐ Heavy

Light

Description _____

_____

Overall _____ /10 _____   Recommend   Yes / No

Experience _____

_____

_____

Dispensary (name/location) _____

Strain _____ indica ☐ Price _____ $/g
                                  sativa ☐

Color
☐ Dark

☐ Light

Clarity
☐ Opaque

☐ Clear

Cannabis Scent
Heavy ☐ ☐ ☐ ☐

Light

Pine/Earthy Citrus Skunk/Cheese Floral

Description
_____

_____

Taste

Floral Citrus
Fruity   Cheese
Peppery   Nutty
    Spicy Earthy

Cannabis Flavor
☐ Heavy

Light

Description
_____

_____

Overall _____ /10 _____   Recommend Yes / No

Experience
_____

_____

Date _____

Dispensary (name/location) _____

Strain _____ indica ☐ Price _____ $/g
                                  sativa ☐

Color
☐ Dark

☐ Light

Clarity
☐ Opaque

☐ Clear

Cannabis Scent
Heavy ☐ ☐ ☐ ☐
Light

Pine/Earthy *Citrus* *Skunk/Cheese* *Floral*

Description _____

_____

Taste

Floral *Citrus*
Fruity   *Cheese*
Peppery   *Nutty*
Spicy *Earthy*

Cannabis Flavor
☐ Heavy

☐ Light

Description _____

_____

Overall _____ /10 _____   Recommend   Yes / No

Experience _____

_____

_____

Date _____

Dispensary (name/location) _____

Strain _____ indica ☐ Price _____ $/g
                                sativa ☐

Color
☐ Dark
☐ Light

Clarity
☐ Opaque
☐ Clear

Cannabis Scent
Heavy ☐ ☐ ☐ ☐
Light
Pine/Earthy *Citrus* *Skunk/Cheese* *Floral*

Description _____

_____

Taste
Floral Citrus
Fruity   Cheese
Peppery   Nutty
Spicy Earthy

Cannabis Flavor
☐ Heavy
  Light

Description _____

_____

Overall _____ /10 _____   Recommend   Yes / No

Experience _____

_____

_____

Date _____

Dispensary (name/location) _____

Strain _____   indica ☐   Price _____ $/g
                                      sativa ☐

Color
☐ Dark
☐ Light

Clarity
☐ Opaque
☐ Clear

Cannabis Scent
Heavy ☐ ☐ ☐ ☐
Light
Pine/Earthy *Citrus* *Skunk/Cheese* *Floral*

Description _____
_____

Taste

Floral Citrus
Fruity   Cheese
Peppery   Nutty
Spicy Earthy

Cannabis Flavor
☐ Heavy
☐ Light

Description _____
_____

Overall _____ /10   Recommend   Yes / No

Experience _____
_____
_____

I hope you enjoyed "working" your way through this journal.

May this be an addition to many volumes of

The **Chronnoisseur**

in your collection!